Grief and Adjustment to Change:

A no-nonsense approach

Avigail Abarbanel

Fully Human Psychotherapy
http://fullyhuman.co.uk

Grief and Adjustment to Change: A no-nonsense approach

(Booklet 1 in the *Fully Human Psychotherapy Tools for Life Series*)

Other booklets in the series:

- *Don't Put Up With Anxiety: Cure it!*
- *Trauma & Its Impact: What you need to know*

First published on Amazon Kindle 2017
(Latest update 25th January 2019)

Table of Contents

Introduction

> "A person removed from his own room, almost without preparation and transition, and set upon the height of a great mountain range, would feel ... an unparalleled insecurity, and abandonment to something inexpressible would almost annihilate him. He would think himself falling or hurled out into space or exploded into a thousand pieces: what a monstrous lie his brain would have to invent to catch up with and explain the state of his senses!" – Rainer Maria Rilke *Letters to a Young Poet*.

Rilke was a poet, not a brain researcher but he was able to capture so well the magnitude of the shock that our brain goes through after a major life change.

Change is an inseparable part of life and we live in a time of especially rapid change. Everyone knows that. But what people usually don't know so well is how change affects us. People think in terms of 'coping' with change, and 'coping well' with change is seen as a sign of personal strength or character, while 'not coping' is seen as weakness, or a personal failure.

In our society 'coping'[1] can mean 'getting on with it', 'not making a fuss' and certainly not complaining no matter bad the situation is and how long it lasts. People expect themselves (and are expected by others), to continue to function as they always have, regardless of the type or magnitude of the change they have just been through. Even after bereavement I hear clients say things like: "But it's been six weeks already. Shouldn't I be fine by now? Why am I still feeling so low?" This uninformed attitude comes at a great cost to us individually and as a society.

This booklet is based on a paper that I originally wrote in 2003 and that was intended for GPs. Doctors are often the first point of contact for people when they feel low, stressed or anxious, when they find it

---

[1] I don't like the word 'cope'. I think it means putting up with a bad situation. Sometimes it is necessary to persevere through something unpleasant or difficult. However, to be well, we should ideally only put up with bad situations for short periods of time. Everyone deserves much more out of life than just coping.

hard to function or when they worry about how they feel. My paper was meant to help GPs think differently about some of the emotional experiences that patients were worried about.

I wrote the paper out of concern that when people told GPs they were unhappy GPs tended to jump to the conclusion that they were depressed. More than three quarters of the client I have been seeing over many years of practice who come in with a GP diagnosis of depression are not depressed at all. As a psychotherapist I have always found this worrying and I believe everyone should be concerned about this.

In order to deal with problems in any area of life, we need to understand the problem correctly. You can't offer appropriate or relevant help or treatment if you get a situation wrong. No GP would diagnose a medical condition and prescribe treatment without carrying out appropriate tests. Misdiagnosis is likely to lead to the wrong treatment. This is not only unhelpful. It can be disastrous. For reasons I don't understand there seem to be different rules in place when it comes to people's psychological health. Most GPs never use any kind of diagnostic tool for depression [2] but are as quick to use the label 'depression' with patients and prescribe serious medication.

What GPs often miss is the fact that a lot of the patients who are unhappy, anxious or stressed, are likely to have experienced one or more major life changes. They do not understand that their patients are going through a natural process of adjustment to these major changes. Nor do they understand the way these changes are affecting those patients.

I wanted GPs to understand what happens to our brain when we go through one or more big life changes. I wanted them to start asking their patients about any big changes they have been through and to be able to reassure and advise them appropriately. People are already frightened enough by what they are experiencing. But instead of reassurance most GPs tend to frighten patients even more by giving them the label of 'depression'. In many cases they inappropriately prescribe powerful mind-altering medication for anxiety or depression or both.

---

[2] There are diagnostic tools for depression available to GPs but they are rarely used.

My paper did not go far with GPs but when I started to hand copies of it to clients and their family members the reaction surprised me. The feedback I received was that the paper was clear, that it made sense and that it was greatly reassuring. People have always said they felt relief when they read it.

I kept working on this paper over the years. I have expanded and improved it and it has proven to be helpful to people from all walks of life. After all these years I thought it was time for it to be published as a booklet so it can be available more widely.

If you are grieving or adjusting to a significant life change make sure that others in your life read this booklet too. They are likely to be much more understanding and patient with what you are going through, and hopefully also more helpful and supportive.

There are stages in life when change is naturally more frequent and more dramatic. I believe that young people and the elderly could benefit from knowing more about their process of adjusting to change. People who have reached retirement go through massive life changes and so do young adults just leaving home for the first time to go to university, to offer but two examples.

Understanding what change means to our brain, how it affects us and knowing what to expect, can go a long way towards preventing unnecessary worry. It can prevent people from feeling they are 'failing' or 'going crazy' or that they are weak. Children too should have no problem understanding what this booklet is discussing. It would help if an adult, a teacher or a parent, can discuss the process of grief and adjustment to change with children and young people and answer any questions they have. It will help reassure them that what they are feeling in the face of so much change in their life is OK and that it will pass by itself once their brain has finished doing what nature has designed it to do.

I hope you will find this booklet helpful and reassuring. I welcome comments, feedback and questions, so feel free to write to me. My contact details are on my website at: http://fullyhuman.co.uk

What is grief?

Everything about us is processed in the brain. Psychology is not an 'airy fairy' or abstract thing. Our psychology, how we are, what we feel, think, believe, how we experience the world and ourselves and how we change are all a result of processes that are happening inside our brain.

If you understand this you would also see that there is nothing mysterious about grief. Grief is a physiological (and therefore psychological) process that our brain goes through after any significant life change.

Like all mammals our brain must maintain an internal image or representation of the environment and reality we live in. We do not interact with the world directly, but rather through the circuitry inside our brain. When an important change happens in our life, our external reality can change quite dramatically and quickly, but our brain needs time to adjust its internal 'picture' of our reality. This internal image of our world is embedded in neural networks that need to be updated. New brain cells, new connections, and new neural networks and circuitry take time to build or update. They don't happen straight way, or over night. This is the reason why we don't just adjust to change instantaneously, or why we can't learn a new skill or language overnight.

Without an up-to-date internal image of their environment all animals are vulnerable to danger. If they do not know for sure where the food, water or shelter are, where predators might lurk or what other dangers or threats might be in their environment, they could end up being someone's lunch, get injured, or die of hunger or thirst. Since our mammal brain, (our limbic system) is responsible for keeping us alive it will feel just as vulnerable after a major change as the brain of any animal.

It doesn't matter that we no longer live in jungles and among predators. Without adjusting to a big life change we cannot function properly in our post-change reality. Our brain would consider us to be in mortal danger. This is why our brain considers adjustment to change a *top priority survival task*, and why most of us feel so vulnerable, scared and exposed during grief.

> Grief is a neurological (brain) process
> of adjusting to a significant life change.
> Adjustment to change is a top-priority survival task
> in all animals including humans

Each human brain is unique. How long it takes to adjust varies from one individual to another. It will depend on the particular brain and also on the nature, magnitude and significance of the change to that particular parson. We can't do much about the basic quality of our brains and we often have little control over how big or important the change is. But the length of grief or adjustment and how it feels can depend on how well we accommodate it, and there is a lot we can do about that!

I choose to expand the use of the word 'grief', usually associated with loss, to cover this process of adjustment to change. In a seminar I once gave on this topic some of my colleagues were uncomfortable with the fact that I was using the word 'grief' in this way. I am happy to consider alternatives, but I haven't yet had any suggestions. So for the time being, I use these terms, 'grief' and 'adjustment to change', interchangeably. This also means that I think of grief as much more than a *sad* response to loss, although loss and sadness are often a part of the process of adjustment.

There is no point fighting, reasoning, medicating or attempting to eliminate or 'heal' this process because it is a basic and necessary survival neurological (brain) task, and not an illness or a pathology. Although the adjustment process often feels awful (I talk about it in more detail later in this booklet) it is natural and necessary. Frankly we don't really have much of a choice about it. It comes with having the brain we have. To fight the adjustment process or to try to eliminate it is not only impossible, it is also as senseless as fighting the fact that we need sleep, food, water or to empty our bowels and bladder regularly. We will not only fail if we tried to fight these natural needs. We will also risk doing serious harm to ourselves. Our basic life functions come with the body and the brain we have and they are part of our regular maintenance. We need to do is understand this and learn how to help the process instead of fighting and resisting it.

> Grief or adjustment to change is not an illness, pathology or a sign of something going wrong. It is a basic survival task that the brain must go through after any big life change.

Grief or depression?

As I mentioned in the introduction, I have been alarmed by the number of clients who come to my practice with a diagnosis of depression, and who in fact turn out not to be depressed at all. People who don't suffer from depression but are unhappy could be undergoing an adjustment to one or more big changes. When people complain about feeling bad, most people and even GPs and mental health professionals tend to not ask what changes they have been through in the previous few weeks, months or years.

Some of the symptoms of grief can look similar to depression, but the process of grief is quite different from depression. One of my clients once made the insightful observation that depression is stagnant and has no energy in it. Grief on the other hand is a dynamic process that tends to have a sense of movement about it.

Depression is usually a result of being in a bad situation or feeling bad for a long time and not having the ability to improve our situation. It's an experience of powerlessness and of being trapped. For example, children who are living in a bad situation and are unable to get away or get help from anywhere, would suffer on and off from depression that they can carry into their adult life.

Unlike depression, grief, while intensely uncomfortable, is energetic and dynamic. It's because it is a process of *updating* our inner brain reality from the image of *what used to be*, to what *is now*. Grief moves us from the past, from the world as it was *before* the change, to the present, the reality as it is now *after* the change.

As a psychotherapist I do generally think that anti-depressants are over-prescribed. They are offered too often to anyone who happens to feel 'bad', low or have uncomfortable feelings. I have heard from a few of my clients that a GP has offered them anti-depressants for back pain, because antidepressants can act as muscle relaxants. Even if it is true that they can, is it wise to give people potentially addictive medication intended for depression that can have a strong effect on the brain and sometimes serious side effects, for back pain?

My point is that grief or adjustment to change is not depression. It's therefore not appropriate and not helpful to offer medication designed for depression, to a person who is going through a natural, normal, and necessary update of their neural circuitry because of a significant life change. What people really need is to understand the process they are going through be reassured that it's normal and that it will pass.

Blocking grief

Grief or adjustment to a big change is a process that needs to be experienced fully. There are no shortcuts. It's just how our brain is... Emotions must not be blocked or interrupted because they are a part of the physical integration or 'upgrade' work that the brain is doing.

In order for the adjustment process to progress and complete itself fully and successfully, some uncomfortable feelings have to be felt. Any drug, prescription medication, alcohol, caffeine, sugar, nicotine or any behaviour that people use to try and *numb* or *medicate* their emotions during grief are likely to do them harm in the long term. This is because avoiding the feelings we feel during adjustment to change can have the effect of *blocking or slowing down* the process. Blocking grief or adjustment comes at a great cost because it means that we do not adjust properly to our new reality. We therefore cannot be fully present or function properly in our present reality.

The implications of un-grieved or blocked grief can be serious. I see a lot of this in my practice. People who do not grieve or adjust properly after one or several life changes do not acclimatise properly to their new reality. Their neurological and therefore their mental 'landscape' (the neural networks responsible for holding an image of their reality) is not up-to-date with their present (post-change) life circumstances. Their mind is essentially out of step with the actual reality they live in.

Blocked grief or adjustment can lead to ongoing anxiety, a sense of aimlessness, feeling lost, inability to make plans for the future, inability to participate in relationships properly and a feeling of moving through life like a zombie just surviving from moment to moment but not really living. People who block grief risk compromising the quality of their life, and quite often they suffer from physical symptoms. If grief is blocked for long enough, it can sometimes lead to depression. But this kind of depression usually lifts fairly quickly once the unfinished or blocked grief underneath it is acknowledged and accommodated.

Having said all of that, I do understand why in some situations people would resist their adjustment or grief process. Everyone knows instinctively that allowing the process to complete itself means coming to terms with the change or the loss they have suffered. There are times when people do not want to come to terms with their loss or change. How can we seriously ask a refugee parent to accept and come to terms with the fact that all of their children drowned while fleeing a war zone? How do you ever get over something like this? Losing a child is one of the worst losses anyone can suffer. How can we judge anyone who doesn't want to come to terms with losing someone they love, losing their entire way of life or accepting a disability?

As a therapist I do not judge people who resist the process of adjustment. I understand this resistance. Nevertheless, not adjusting comes with a heavy cost to our wellbeing and our relationships. If people still choose to not adjust despite understanding the cost, they have to be respected for making this choice.

Change and the brain

Grief is the process that builds a 'bridge' to take us from the world as we knew it before the change to the world as it is now. Grief helps us move from reality '**A**' before the change — when everything was familiar and therefore we felt safe — to reality '**B**', which is what the world is like now after the change, new, unfamiliar, unknown, strange and therefore (from our ancient mammal's brain point of view) unsafe!

The road from reality **A** to reality **B** is deeply troubling and uncomfortable. It is what we *feel* and *experience* as the process of grief or adjustment to change. We can feel uncertain, out of step with our life, responsibilities and relationships, vulnerable, confused, lost, purposeless, unsafe and afraid.

The diagram on the next page tries to show that it's uncomfortable and scary when you are building a bridge at the same time as you are walking on it. You don't feel certain that the next section will be there for you because there is no complete bridge yet. It can feel as if the next step will plunge you into an abyss. Still, it's taking that next step that actually builds the next section of the bridge. The point is that walking on a bridge while you are building it feel incredibly insecure and even crazy.

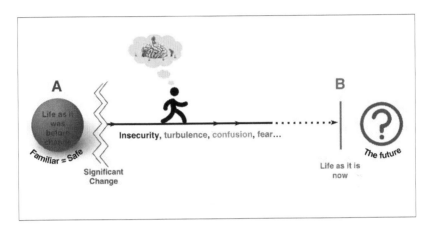

The process of grief is *physiological*. You are not imagining it. Building new brain connections and neural networks is extremely tiring, physically and mentally. The process uses up a great deal of energy, and doesn't leave much for other things. It is similar to when a computer is used for a massive computational task but we still try to do a bit of word processing on the side. It's going to be clunky and slow and things are not going to work as well as when the entire system and its power are available to us. It is simply very busy.

One of the uncomfortable effects of this heavy processing is that the data from our senses are going to feel different to the usual. So for example, if you are used to feeling deep pleasure at the sound of a particular piece of music, you might feel little or nothing while you are adjusting to change. Flavours, smells, physical sensations, sights, anything coming from the senses will not feel the same as before the change. There is just not enough 'computational' power (mental energy or 'juice') in the brain for us to receive the full effect of what our senses are picking up from the environment. Life is likely to feel duller and we just will not be our usual selves.

One of the biggest problems with grief and adjustment to change is that we have no choice but to continue to use the same brain *while* it is going through the adjustment. It would have been so much easier if we could put our adjusting brain in a box and use a spare brain while the other one is adjusting. It's like when your car is being fixed at the garage and they lend you a courtesy car to minimise the discomfort of not having a car. It doesn't work like that when it comes to our brain. But this is one of the main reasons that life during grief is so difficult.

Because our brain considers adjustment to change vital to our survival it will make it a top priority task. It will always attempt to allocate as much energy and resources as possible to the adjustment process. This is because from our brain's point of view we are in danger as long as our mental image of reality doesn't match our actual reality. Everything else that we have to do just has to take a back seat.

Our brain doesn't care that we have to work, study, sit exams, write essays, raise children, pay bills, drive cars, run businesses, care for others, participate in relationships, cook, clean our house, socialise, keep our job and do the shopping. In today's reality most of us have a lot to do and to accomplish. Everyone's life is filled with responsibilities and commitments but during the adjustment process our brain will not leave us enough energy to function as we usually do. This can leave many people feeling inadequate or as if they are letting themselves or others down.

People don't realise it but having a big brain takes up a lot of our energy. In his book *Sapiens: A Brief History of Humankind*, Dr Yuval Harari says:

> "The fact is that a jumbo brain is a jumbo drain on the body. It's not easy to carry around, especially when encased inside a massive skull. It's even harder to fuel. It accounts for about 2–3 per cent of total body weight, but it consumes 25 per cent of the body's energy when the body is at rest. By comparison, the brains of other apes require only 8 per cent of rest-time energy."

In other words, even when we are not adjusting to a change it takes up a great deal of our physical energy to just maintain our brain. This gets much worse during grief or at any time when the brain is busy building or updating neural networks (such as when we are learning something new or are going through a new experience).

Think of how many hours newborns, toddlers and even small children sleep in a day or how tired you can feel when you learn something new. This is because the brain is busy. It is working physically hard to create new neural pathways and networks to accommodate a huge amount of new information, skills, knowledge, abilities and so on. Whenever the brain goes through a period of more intense building and updating we are going to be more tired than usual and will not function at the usual level we expect to when our brain is not adjusting.

When do we grieve?

Many assume that a change has to be 'bad' or 'negative' in order to trigger grief. But the truth is that we need to adjust in response to *any* significant change, good or bad, desirable or undesirable, planned or unplanned.

We adjust to small changes all the time. But because small everyday changes are not necessarily linked to our survival the process doesn't take long and we might not feel more than slight fluctuations in our mood or our performance. Significant changes are those that our brain associates with survival. There the process is more demanding on the brain and therefore physically and psychologically more difficult.

Our very sense of what we think of as sanity *depends* on having an inside image that matches the outside. If you see someone on the street (who isn't a mime) chasing butterflies that aren't there or talking to themselves you'd probably think of him or her as insane. That individual sees butterflies in his or her head and is having a conversation with someone only they can see.

While we are adjusting to a change we can all feel a little 'insane'. That's because our internal image of reality is in fact out of step with our actual reality. We can still see and experience things, people or situations that are no longer there in the real world but are still wired into our brain.

The grief or adjustment process will attempt to begin almost immediately after any change if the change is significant enough to require an update of our internal picture of the world (our neural circuitry). Adjustment can sometimes begin in *anticipation* of a big change as we begin to imagine what our life would look like after it happens. This can happen for example, when you know someone is going to die, when you are about to move house, when a baby is about to be born, when you are about to change jobs or move countries.

Here are some examples of life changes that are followed by grief:

- Losing someone significant to death or another transition.
- Losing someone to suicide.
- Abandonment by someone significant (at any age).
- Losing a pet.
- Loss of a friendship or any significant relationship where we were relatively strongly attached.
- Infidelity or any betrayal.
- Moving or relocating by choice.
- Dislocation as a result of war or of being driven out of one's home, city, country.
- Losing a house e.g., due to natural disaster or financial misfortune.
- A house break-in and burglary.
- Starting, ending, or changing jobs or careers.
- Retirement.
- Workplace restructuring or changes in management and leadership at work.
- Changes in rules or values in the workplace.
- Acquiring new information that causes a major shift in perspective (e.g. uncovering an important family secret or a secret about one's community or group).
- Office refitting or relocation.
- Loss of a business.
- House renovations.
- Having surgery (including cosmetic surgery or other elective procedures).
- Being diagnosed with an illness.
- Losing a part of the body, an ability, a sense or a function due to injury, illness, medical procedure or age.
- Falling in love.
- Getting married.
- Divorce or end of a relationship, family breakup.
- Giving birth.
- Becoming a parent through birth of a child, adoption, fostering or having stepchildren.

- Any significant change in lifestyle.
- Birth of a child with a disability.
- A child's accident, injury, diagnosis of illness or a child acquiring a disability.
- Not becoming a parent, e.g., discovering infertility, or not having had the opportunity to become a parent.
- Miscarriage or pregnancy termination. Grief after a termination can affect men as well as women.
- Becoming a carer to someone close.
- Being or having been a victim of any form of abuse, attack, political persecution or a crime.
- Leaving a cult or any other type of close-knit religious, social or political group.
- Being, or having been a victim of a natural disaster.
- Starting and finishing kindergarten, school, apprenticeship, university or military service.
- Going through early childhood (childhood involves non-stop change and adjustment.)
- Moving from childhood to adolescence (adolescence also involves ongoing change and adjustment.)
- Moving from adolescence to adulthood. (Early adulthood can involve many important life changes in rapid succession before we settle down more a bit later.)
- Leaving home.
- Starting university or college.
- Learning something new e.g., a new profession, a language, or a set of skills.
- Menopause and other signs of ageing.
- Going on holidays or going overseas.
- Process of recovering from trauma, e.g., in therapy.
- Changes to self/identity and to perception of self.
- Discovering a new sexual orientation.
- Disclosing a new sexual orientation (coming out).
- Gender reassignment.
- Giving up on or getting over an addiction — e.g., smoking, alcoholism, gambling, an eating disorder.

- Loss of a dream or expectation. (The brain needs to adjust even when our *imagined* dreams, expectations or plans do not happen or do not happen as we hope or expect.)
- Any other life change (positive or negative) that requires a significant adjustment.

Because people tend to associate grief with a negative life experience it can be shocking and disturbing when something positive that they were looking forward to finally happens and they find themselves feeling awful. This can lead people to assume wrongly that they have made a mistake, that they were wrong in their decision to marry, move house, renovate, give up on an addiction, have a child, start a university degree, leave home or accept that new position.

Many new mothers and fathers tend to feel like failures simply because no one explained or warned them about the adjustment they will be going to go through after the birth of their child. The birth of a child is a massive life change that affects people's reality on many levels. If new parents do not understand that their brains are adjusting they can panic and try to block the process.

Many new parents worry unnecessarily that they are not good enough parents because they feel so awful, irritable, impatient, angry, or sad. They fear that they don't love their child enough, that they can't function the way they think they should, or that others might judge them if they knew how they really felt. They think they 'should' be happy and can judge themselves for not feeling that way. (I do wonder sometimes how much of Postnatal Depression is really adjustment to change!)

Feeling like this following a change that is expected to be a happy one can make life even more difficult than it needs to be. It can also prolong the grief process unnecessarily. It doesn't help that many parents are expected to take care of newborn babies all by themselves. Given the big adjustment that parenting requires and the time the parents' brain can take to adjust it would be so much more helpful if there was a community of non-anxious, well informed, and safe people around the parents to support them as their brains do the adjustment to their new lifestyle, role and identity.

I believe that a lot of unnecessary suffering can be prevented if people understood the adjustment process their brain goes through, and were taught to be patient with it, and protect it. My clients still have to go through the discomfort, confusion and pain of grief or adjustment, but most feel enormous relief when they realise that what they are going through is just 'normal'. Grief is difficult enough on its own without having to also suffer from fear of going crazy, from worry that there is something wrong with your mind or from shame or guilt for not adjusting to a new reality straight away, and not being your usual self.

Reflection

• How many significant life changes have you been through in the past few weeks, months, year, two years, five years or longer?

• It might be a good idea to make a list just to see it more clearly. It might surprise you. Be sure to list all changes. Don't discriminate between positive or negative ones. A change is a change and all significant changes require the brain to adjust.

• Have you ever acknowledged these changes?

• What did it feel like when these changes happened?

• Do you think you have adjusted to those changes? Is it possible you are still adjusting?

• What is the difference between how you feel/felt during the grief/adjustment process and how you feel/felt once the adjustment has finished?

The symptoms of grief

The list below is based on what clients have reported to me over the years and on my observations of myself. It is obviously not an exhaustive list because everyone is unique and there are as many experiences as there are people. You might want to add to the list or adjust items based on your experience.

I have divided the symptoms into categories that made sense to me. But I am aware that the division isn't perfect and that some symptoms might appear in more than one category. Not all the symptoms apply to everyone and not all of them will appear together.

Despite what you might have heard or read elsewhere there are in fact no well-defined chronological stages to grief or adjustment. Anything can happen at any time until the adjustment is complete. Grief can feel like it moves in waves or it might feel like a roller coaster, like being shaken or like being sucked into a swamp or a black hole.

Until the adjustment is complete we can feel like we have regressed and are going backwards and forwards a lot. We will have 'good days' and 'bad days'. You know that the grief is nearing its completion when you wake up one morning and feel well rested for the first time in a while.

In terms of brain functioning grief is similar to any process of learning. When we first learn something new we are unreliable. Sometimes we do really well and sometimes we slip right back to ignorance or clumsiness and make mistakes. We become reliable and master our new skill or knowledge only when the brain has finished connecting the necessary neural pathways and has created the neural networks required for us to have the new skill.

When this has been achieved we feel confident again and we will be skilled and knowledgeable in our new area. There will be an ease and confidence about our new skill or knowledge. Similarly, in grief and adjustment we begin to feel back to 'normal' only when the brain has completed the adjustment or upgrade of the relevant neural circuitry. Only then we will feel like the 'clouds have parted', 'the sun is out again', that we are back to being ourselves again, our thoughts are clearer and we are comfortable and safe again in our reality. Everything is likely to feel simpler, brighter and lighter.

Emotional symptoms of grief

- Numbness – Numbness can come and go at any point during the process.
- Shock
- Feeling unsettled
- Confusion
- Sadness
- Pain

- Regret
- Stress
- Restlessness and agitation
- Impatience
- Feelings of isolation and loneliness – These can come from feeling that no one can understand what you are going through, or from the actual experience of people not being patient or understanding.
- Emotional 'heaviness'. Everything feels difficult.
- Feeling out of control.
- Feeling like you can't cope even with things that at other times are simple or easy for you to do.
- Anger, irritability and unusually short temper.
- Fear
- A sense of dissatisfaction with life.
- Anxiety and fear about the process itself and the physical symptoms that can accompany it.
- Fear of appearing weak to others.
- Guilt or shame – e.g., about not performing as well as usual, about being a burden on others, or not being able to be there for others as you normally would.
- Low levels of emotions and a diminished ability to experience pleasure or joy.
- Diminished interest in sex and sometimes in physical contact in general.
- People with pre-existing trauma often have their trauma symptoms triggered during grief.

Mental symptoms of grief

- Impairment of the short-term memory
- Diminished concentration and attention span
- Absent-mindedness, forgetfulness, feeling distracted
- A tendency to focus on the negative aspects of life, and often a sense that everything is going wrong.
- Loss of interest in what was previously of great interest.
- Difficulty in dealing with responsibilities.

- Fear of going 'crazy'.
- Difficulty making decisions.
- Feeling stupid.
- Inability to think about the future and make plans.
- Worrying about not achieving or not living up to usual standards.
- Worrying that you will never feel good again and will always feel the way you do now.
- Just worrying about everything.
- Feeling like even simple, ordinary tasks are too much.

Physical symptoms of grief

- Complete exhaustion regardless of the amount of sleep you get.
- Changes in appetite – loss of appetite, erratic appetite or overeating for comfort.
- Sleep disturbances – interrupted sleep, not being able to fall asleep or needing to sleep more than usual.
- Changes in dream patterns.
- Anxiety symptoms and increase in the likelihood of anxiety and panic attacks.
- Increased tendency towards allergies.
- A variety of often non-life-threatening medical symptoms where there are no physical causes or they are inconclusive.
- Aches and pains with no serious physical causes.
- Loss of sensitivity in some of the senses. Flavours, colours or sounds can seem dull compared with the usual. Eyesight can get worse temporarily.

Relational symptoms of grief

- Reduced enjoyment from social contacts and activities.
- Tendency toward introversion, or closing off. Needing more time in solitude than at other times.
- Low tolerance for the company of others. (After five minutes of being even with your best friend you just want to be alone.)
- Need to talk a lot.
- Impatience with people who are needy or dependent.

- Needing the company of non-anxious and non-needy people who can be supportive.
- Impaired ability to feel empathy and to listen to others.
- Not caring so much about what is happening in the life of others or in the world, even if normally you tend to be a caring and generous person.
- Tendency to feel like a burden on others.
- Diminished interest in sex.
- Annoyance with partner that isn't justified by anything in particular that he or she does.
- Feelings of disappointment in your relationship because of the perception that your partner cannot understand what you are going through, or that he or she isn't feeling the same way as you.
- Worrying that your partner will be impatient with what you are going through.
- Tendency towards marital or relationship tensions, fighting or distance as a result of all the above.

Behavioural symptoms of grief

- Crying – but not everyone cries or cries a lot. Some people don't cry at all and some cry but only when they are alone.

- Increase in tendency to withdraw.

- Increase in likelihood of substance abuse such as alcohol, drugs and even prescription medication or other addictive or compulsive behaviour – these can be ways by which the person is trying to numb or soothe or cope with their internal chaos, anxiety and discomfort.

- Increase in likelihood of violent behaviour or abuse of others if the person already has these tendencies. People who are abusive do not cope with stress or anxiety well. Their behaviour can be their way of expressing what they feel. This is unacceptable and others must not put up with such behaviour. If the person is grieving he or she should be given the right guidance and support but not be allowed to victimise others.

- Tendency to take emotional distress out on others who are close to the grieving person such as children, partners or work colleagues. This is also unacceptable.

- Increase in the likelihood of risk-taking behaviours. This can be more common in adolescents and young people but some adults will display this symptom as well.

- Becoming hyper-active or trying to do too much. This can be used as a distraction from the feelings or as a way of trying to prove to yourself and others that you are 'OK'.

- It can be difficult to meditate or do any activity that in non-grief times would normally be relaxing.

Spiritual and existential symptoms of grief

- Increase in tendency to worry about the meaning of one's life and place in the world/universe.
- A sense of being lost and losing your sense of direction or meaning.
- A tendency to focus on the negatives everywhere and in everyone.
- More thoughts than usual about illness and death.
- Thoughts and worries about the state of the world.
- A sense of facing a void or an abyss.
- Loss of touch with, or confusion about, one's spirituality.
- Anger with God, self or life.
- Difficulty or inability to feel a sense of peace and wellbeing.

Supporting grief / adjustment

There are things that we and others can do that support the process of adjustment and things that can get in the way of it. I list below some of the things I believe we need and that are helpful and some of the things we don't need and that are unhelpful. What I mean by helpful or unhelpful is to do with helping the process move along naturally. I do not mean 'fixing' it or 'healing' it. Remember that adjustment is a natural and necessary brain process and not a problem to be fixed.

What we need most during grief/adjustment to change

- **Time and lots of it** – As I mentioned earlier, the length and intensity of grief will vary from one individual to another. Everyone's brain is different and will take a different amount of time to adjust. Therefore we can't put a time limit on grief. Each brain takes its own time to develop the neural connections and networks it needs. (I usually tell my clients that grief takes as long as it takes but usually not as long as they think it will.)

- **A lot of rest and sleep** – One of the most obvious signs of grief is total exhaustion. The brain is working hard and people will feel bone tired regardless of how long they sleep. During sleep the brain is free to focus on the processing it needs to do, without being bothered by outside sensory input. Therefore a lot of daytime naps can help us move quicker through the adjustment process. (One of the signs that you are coming out of your grief is when you wake up one morning and for the first time in a while you feel rested.)

- **The company of non-anxious and non-needy people** – During grief we have very little 'brain space', or mental and physical energy for anything other than our own adjustment process. People who are anxious and needy can be draining at any time. During grief they can be unbearable. They don't know how to be with others without having their needs and emotions 'spilling out' everywhere. Spending too much time around such people during grief can be a block to your adjustment.

- **Acknowledgment and validation** – We need to hear and be reminded that what we are feeling is OK. This is because most of us have been brought up without validation of our emotional experience, so we tend to worry that what we feel is unacceptable to others.

- **Time in solitude and permission to take it** – Even otherwise extraverted people can feel quite introverted during grief. Introverted people usually need more time in solitude than extraverted people in order to replenish their energy. During grief it's important that you give yourself the quiet time that your brain might need in order to process the adjustment. Remember you also do not have the 'brain space' for much anyway. Let others know that you need more time alone than usual.

- **As little responsibility as possible** – Because during grief we are not functioning to our normal standards or capacity it's hard to cope with responsibilities. Even things that are otherwise easy to do are hard during grief. You really don't need too much responsibility so if possible don't take on anything new and allow yourself to do less. It will be temporary and you will get back to your usual self when the process is complete.

- **Practical help (not advice)** – During grief and adjustment, people need practical help to manage and cope with their responsibilities and commitments. Their brain is busy and doesn't have the usual resources. Even simple routine tasks can feel like too much. It's OK and often necessary to ask for help. It's only temporary. When you are adjusted to the change, your brain will go back to its normal functioning.

- **Strategies to cope with daily routine** – Forgetfulness and distraction are common during grief and it is easy to misplace or lose things. People need to pay extra attention during driving, operating complicated or dangerous equipment or otherwise facing complex and responsible tasks. Making lists and reducing workload can help a lot to keep better track of things and pace yourself.

What we *do not* need during grief/adjustment to change

- 'Strategies' to make us 'feel better', advice or any other attempts to change how we feel or what we think such as a 'different perspective' on what had happened.
- Antidepressants or any other mind-altering drugs like alcohol for example.
- Heavy exercise.
- Demanding timetables, schedules or deadlines.

- The company of people who are anxious, needy, insensitive or otherwise emotionally unskilled and who might be impatient with our grief and demanding our energy.
- Any unnecessary input that might distract the brain from its main task, and might take away essential mental energy that's needed to build the new neural pathways and networks.

Good quality grief therapy/counselling

Seeing a therapist during grief can be a good idea. Because everyone's life experience is unique and every brain is unique grief is naturally a lonely experience. No one, even with the best of intentions, can know exactly what it's like for someone else when they are adjusting to an important life change.

To help the brain process better some people might need to talk a lot. Talking can help the brain process and integrate neural pathways and create new neural networks. It is common for many people to feel that they are becoming a burden on their friends and family because they are talking a lot about the change and need to go over the same things many times. When you see a therapist, you don't have to feel guilty or worry that you are a bother or a burden. It's the therapist's job to be there for you, listen to you in a helpful way and support you.

There is another important reason for seeing a therapist. A recent process of grief can often trigger older unfinished grieves from the past. These are adjustments you haven't yet completed properly. Everyone has a few of those. A new change can also trigger other 'unfinished business' you might have inside your brain that you might not even be fully conscious of. Having a counsellor there to support you can help you process other issues that might come up as you experience and process your more recent experience of adjustment to change.

Grief can be a great (if uncomfortable) 'university' to learn to interact with your emotions better and get to know your inner world. A good therapist can help you make use of your grief process to grow and to develop better emotional skills.

Among other things good grief counsellor should be able to provide you with

- **Reassurance** – that what you are going through is normal and will pass.

- **Validation and recognition** – of your feelings, thoughts and body sensations. Do not allow your therapist to try and change how you feel.

- **Information and education** about the grief process.

- An opportunity to **identify, explore and remove blocks** to grief.

- **Strategies or suggestions to accommodate the grief process** in case you have to work or care for others while grieving.

- **Strategies or suggestions to care for your body**, for example: an emphasis on a healthy diet and vitamin supplements to strengthen/boost the immune system, gentle exercise such as gentle forms of yoga and relaxation or Tai Chi, or gentle outdoor walks, reduction or elimination of caffeine and alcohol in your diet, organic meat to reduce hormonal interference, massage.

- **Encouragement to write in a journal**—journaling can be really helpful during grief. It's not for everyone but if it works for you, try it.

- **Gentle spiritual support** – not hard-line or rigid religious 'truths' or practices. Your counsellor should be able to talk with you about your spiritual beliefs, your concerns and your feelings about life, god and what had happened to you. Your counsellor should encourage you to seek other forms of spiritual support and sustenance in case you happen to follow a religion or if you are exploring this area.

- **Referral to a GP** for a general check-up if needed. A good counsellor should encourage you to seek medical advice if you are concerned about something physical.

- Grief therapy should offer you a **rich and flexible environment to express yourself**. Not everyone has well-developed language to describe emotions or their inner world, and not everyone is a 'talker'. Good grief therapy should offer a flexible combination of talking therapy, artwork, play therapy, sand play and other forms of experiential therapy such as psychodrama for example. Even if you normally can talk about your emotions and inner world, during grief it can be hard to verbalise your experiences and your feelings. A flexible and rich experiential therapy environment can offer an opportunity to express yourself safely in other ways.

- Suggestions, opportunities and space for **ceremonies**. Ceremonies can be important during a time of adjustment to a big change. They can provide a symbolic framework for dealing with the change you have been through. They can provide an opportunity to mark the ending or change, create an opportunity for closure or to express yourself in ways that you might find difficult on your own or do not have the background for. Your therapist should be able to make suggestions for ceremonies and be open to your own ideas and wishes about appropriate ceremonies that could be helpful to you and help your grief process along.

Grief and Trauma

People with pre-existing trauma (e.g. trauma from childhood that hasn't been addressed, or hasn't been sufficiently integrated or healed) can feel like they are slipping right into the trauma 'vortex', when they are adjusting to a new change. A change can feel like a major disaster has struck, and it is the end of the world.

Unfortunately, grief and adjustment to change are inseparable from any process of recovery from trauma. Anyone who is working to recover from trauma in therapy for example, will experience a great deal of grief on and off, because for a while they will be constantly adjusting to changes in identity, in perception of reality past, present and future, perception of self and of others, changes in beliefs, in thinking and in feeling. This is one of the reasons that recovery from trauma, compared with therapy for other issues, is so much more challenging and demanding.

> If you know or suspect that you carry childhood trauma *and* you are experiencing a new loss or a big life-change, it might be a good idea to find a good therapist to support you through the process. Don't suffer alone. New grieves throw us back to old unfinished ones, and trauma can be retriggered. There is help out there. (Feel free to show this booklet to your psychotherapist or counsellor if you believe it will help him or her understand better what you are going through.)

Complicated grief

'Complicated grief' is the name we give in my profession to any grief process that doesn't appear to be straightforward. To the best of my knowledge there isn't a clear list of 'symptoms' that describes complicated grief and that distinguishes it from 'ordinary' grief. As a therapist you just know that the client's grief is complicated because it feels somehow more tortured than normal grief, it involves a lot of instability in the person's life and it seems to go on for longer than what you imagine a normal grief should take.

Even if they don't have a name for it, clients usually know instinctively when their grief feels more torturous and more complicated than more straightforward grief. You should listen to your own gut instinct on this and insist that your therapist listens to it as well. People usually don't have a name for this and they tend to think there is something very wrong with them.

Complicated grief can result from a number of possible situations. But there are two common themes behind complicated grief. One is that there is no clear stable reality after the change, so the brain doesn't know what it is it's supposed to adjust to, and two, there are a lot of unsorted 'loose ends' and unfinished things in the reality from before the change.

Straightforward grief would be for example where there has been a death, a burial or cremation and a funeral following a reasonably good relationship, or an amicable divorce or separation between two people who otherwise had a good relationship but made a mutual decision to part ways.

The relationship prior to the death or the separation was straightforward, and the new reality after the change is stable enough, except it's missing the person and the relationship. In such situations the brain has a new and clear reality to adjust to and there are not many unanswered questions. Things were simple, positive and honest, and everything that needed to be said and sorted was said and sorted. Complicated grief is the opposite.

In principle, the more secure the attachment was in the previous situation and the calmer and safer the relationship was, the easier and more straightforward the grief is likely to be. The more insecure the attachment, the more complicated the grief is likely to be.

Paradoxically, children who have had a secure and loving relationship with their parents have a much easier time adjusting and letting go when the parent dies. People whose parents did not offer secure attachment or whose parents were abusive often have a much harder time when the parent dies.

> The more secure the attachment was in the previous situation/relationship, the easier the grief/adjustment is likely to be.
>
> The more insecure the attachment, the more complicated the process will be. This is caused among other things by unfinished business from that relationship or situation, inability to have your point of view seen or acknowledged by others, all the unanswered questions (e.g., 'Why did he / she do this to me?' 'How could he/she do this? 'Why did it happen to me?' 'What did I do wrong?' 'How did I end up in that situation / relationship?' etc.) or inability to see justice done.

I have already mentioned how hard it can be to adjust to any big life change, positive or not, planned or not, desired or not. But there are situations where things 'drag on' maybe because of an illness or maybe because of other circumstances where there is a series of big changes one after another with no end in sight. In these situations the brain cannot adjust to a new stable reality because there isn't one. Reality keeps shifting and changing.

I can imagine that the experience of refugees can be like this or of children growing up with unstable parents, or in cases where children are passed on from one foster carer to another. Reality can continue to shift also in cases of ongoing financial disasters, court cases, a long-term progressive illness (e.g. MS) or any other condition or situation that keeps changing and has no clear end or resolution in sight.

Too much ongoing significant change, especially change that involves serious physical or emotional threat (they often go together) can lead not only to complicated grief. It can, in some people, trigger Post Traumatic Stress (PTS).

The second theme I mentioned in complicated grief is when the relationship or whatever else has changed has been unclear and there are a lot of loose ends, unanswered questions, 'what ifs' and no prospect of getting any kind of acknowledgement, justice or closure. This can happen in relationships or work situations where there has been bullying or abuse but no acknowledgement of the suffering it caused or the aftereffects.

Another example can be bad relationships that break down and are followed by battles in the courts over children or finances. Even if there aren't any custody battles the fact that the two people still share their children or a business they jointly owned can lead to ongoing painful and unstable circumstances.

In such situations the brain will have a hard time adjusting because the person trying to adjust doesn't know when the next 'drama' or disaster would happen, except they know for sure there is going to be one. This is likely to happen to people who have been in a personal or business relationship with someone with a personality disorder.

Other situations where I have seen complicated grief as a result of ongoing change are when people have left cults or otherwise confusing, oppressive, abusive or all-consuming groups, religions or relationships.

As a result of choosing to leave the person might have been slandered, harassed or rejected by their own family, group or circle of friends. I have met clients who had to pick themselves up and move from one city to another a few times in a hurry and leave everything behind, just to get away from a cult or people that kept harassing or pursuing them. The brain will find it difficult to adjust because nothing is stable, at least for a while.

Complicated grief can happen whenever people are left to try to sort things out in their own head after a troubled or torturous situation. It makes it very hard to make sense of things where there is no external validation or acknowledgment of the experience, no answers as to why things happened the way they did, what 'they did wrong', or why they were targeted. People might be judged unfairly, there might be some painful and even traumatic memories and no one to share them with.

Suicide of someone close or a loved-one almost always leads to complicated grief in those left behind, especially where there were no warning signs. Suicide can leave people feeling guilty and confused, and with plenty of unanswered questions. The more violent the suicide, the more traumatic it can be for those left behind.

Complicated grief can reach a resolution. But it can take a lot longer than non-complicated grief and the road to recovery is likely to be windier, 'bumpier', and more painful. It's probably a good idea to work through complicated grief with a skilled and trusted therapist.

As a therapist I often focus initially on supporting people to create as much stability as they can for themselves after a change, as quickly as possible. I advise people against making any further changes where possible, and where they have a choice. It's almost impossible to see things clearly and make good decisions when your brain feels all 'muddled up' and you feel in flux and in emotional pain. But it is a good thing to try to think in the direction of creating stability as quickly as possible. It really is a priority. The more stability there is, the clearer the reality the brain has to adjust to will be.

In my own life, where I can, I try to make sure that I don't leave too much unfinished business between me and others. Not everything is up to me and I don't always have control. But I tell people what I think and what I feel about them regularly so I don't have too many regrets if things end. I don't want to die regretting that I wasn't kind to my partner or that I didn't tell him enough what a difference he made to me and how happy I have been with him. If we wait too long it can be too late. I have had many clients who have found themselves in these situations.

We can work with some of this in therapy and people can heal, but it's always the second-best option. The best option is to get it right where we can.

๛

One thing we can all be sure of is that change is constant. All relationships and all structures we are a part of will end or change at some time or another. It's wise to be well informed about what change does to us and how it makes us feel. It is worth becoming skilled at grieving and adjusting at the same time as trying to not accumulate too many regrets. It will help you and others grieve and adjust more easily and with fewer complications.

I wish no one had to go through this hard, scary and frankly awful process of adjustment each time we experience a significant change. But this is how our brain is built and we don't really have a choice.

Just remember that the grief will pass and you will adjust. If you grieve well you will come out of the process sooner than you imagine, better adjusted to your new reality and probably wiser and more mature than before.

About the author

Avigail Abarbanel has been a psychotherapist in private practice since 1999. She started practicing in Australia and in 2010 moved to the Scottish Highlands. She re-established her practice near Inverness.

Avigail works with individuals, relationships and groups. She is also a trainer, clinical supervisor and writer. Avigail is accredited with the BACP and with COSCA (via the BACP).

Registered Member **16797**
MBACP (Accred)

Visit http://fullyhuman.co.uk for more information about Avigail and her work.

45327451R00021

Printed in Poland
by Amazon Fulfillment
Poland Sp. z o.o., Wrocław